Your Emergency Fund Plan

T.S. AVINI

Your Emergency Fund Plan

Save Smart Without Sacrificing Too Much

by T.S. AVINI

Table of Contents

Chapter 1: Introduction: The Importance of an Emergency Fund

Imagine this: You're driving home from work one day when your car starts to make a peculiar noise. As the sound grows louder, you realize that a visit to the mechanic is inevitable.

Two days later, you're handed a repair estimate far larger than you anticipated. How do you cover this unexpected expense without throwing off your entire budget?.

This is where an emergency fund serves as a financial safety net, one that catches you when life's uncertainties attempt to make you stumble.

In this chapter, we'll examine not only why an emergency fund is necessary but also how it can transform your approach to personal finance.

Why an Emergency Fund is Essential

At its core, an emergency fund is money set aside to cover unexpected expenses, providing financial stability in times of urgent need.

These can range from sudden car repairs and unforeseen medical bills, to job loss or necessary home repairs. The importance of having this fund cannot be overstated—without one, you may find yourself forced to take on debt to manage these surprises, which can affect your financial health for years to come.

The Peace of Mind Factor

One of the greatest non-monetary benefits of an emergency fund is the peace of mind it provides.

Imagine being able to face emergencies without panic, knowing that you have a financial cushion to fall back on. This peace of mind not only reduces stress but also allows you to make decisions more calmly and thoughtfully.

Avoiding Debt Buildup

Without an emergency fund, you might resort to using credit cards or taking loans to cover sudden expenses.

This can quickly spiral into a cycle of debt, as high-interest rates on borrowed money add to your financial burden. An emergency fund is a proactive measure to avoid this trap, ensuring that you can handle surprises without accumulating debt.

Maintaining Financial Goals

Having an emergency fund in place protects your long-term financial goals.

Whether you're saving for your child's education, a future home, or retirement, unexpected expenses won't force you to dip into these pots, thus keeping your plans intact. This fund essentially acts as a guardrail that safeguards your financial roadmap.

How Much Should You Save?

Many people don't realize this, but The general rule of thumb suggests having three to six months' worth of living expenses saved in your emergency fund.

This might seem like a daunting figure at first, but understanding your monthly expenditures and breaking down the savings process into smaller, manageable goals can make this target more approachable.

Step 1: Calculate Your Expenses

Start by calculating your essential monthly expenses, such as rent or mortgage, utilities, groceries, transportation, and insurance.

This will give you a clear idea of how much you need to cover the basics. Multiplying this amount by three to six will provide your emergency fund target.

Step 2: Assess Your Income Stability

If your income is stable and predictable, a fund that covers three months may suffice.

However, if your income is variable—perhaps because you're self-employed or work in a commission-based job—aiming for a six-month safety net might be more prudent.

Step 3: Set Achievable Milestones

Let's not forget, Begin by setting smaller goals. For instance, your first target could be to save one month's worth of expenses.

Once achieved, gradually increase your target to two months, then three, until you reach your final goal. This step-by-step approach makes the process seem less daunting and ensures you can celebrate small victories along the way.

The Components of a Robust Emergency Fund

Creating an effective emergency fund isn't just about stashing cash.

Several factors contribute to its robustness, ensuring that it serves its purpose when the time comes.

Accessibility without Temptation

An emergency fund should be easily accessible, yet separate from your daily checking account to prevent unnecessary spending.

Consider placing it in a dedicated savings account or a money market account that offers easy access while also earning interest. Online banks often provide competitive rates while granting the liquidity needed for emergencies.

Regularly Replenish and Review

Once you've established your emergency fund, commit to reviewing it periodically. Life circumstances change—your expenses might increase, or you might face new responsibilities.

Make it a habit to reassess your fund's adequacy and adjust your saving strategy accordingly. Furthermore, if you do need to dip into this fund, prioritize replenishing it promptly.

Consider Liquidity and Growth Balance

While the primary function of an emergency fund is accessibility, finding a balance between liquidity and growth can enhance its effectiveness.

High-yield savings accounts, for instance, allow your funds to grow modestly, countering inflation while remaining available when needed. Avoid locking your emergency savings in investments or accounts that penalize withdrawals, as these won't serve you readily in a crisis.

Building Your Fund Without Sacrifice

Many individuals hesitate to build an emergency fund due to fear of sacrificing their current lifestyle.

However, saving doesn't have to mean deprivation. By making strategic, small changes, you can steadily build your fund without feeling like you're missing out on life's joys.

Automate Your Savings

Setting up automatic transfers from your checking to your emergency fund can make saving seamless.

Treat this transfer as a non-negotiable expense akin to paying a bill. Over time, you might not even notice the funds leaving your account, yet they'll accumulate steadily in your savings.

Budget Wisely, Spend Thoughtfully

Analyze your spending to identify areas where minor adjustments can lead to significant savings.

Perhaps skipping a few dining out sessions, cutting back on premium TV subscriptions, or opting for a home-brewed coffee can accumulate funds more quickly than you'd expect. The key lies in making choices that align with your priorities and comfort.

Supplement Your Income

Consider finding ways to increase your income for the sole purpose of building your emergency fund.

This could mean taking on freelance work, participating in the gig economy, or selling unused items. Directed earnings from these efforts, even if small, can provide a sizeable boost to your emergency savings.

Conclusion

An emergency fund acts as both a financial cushion and a practical solution to uncertainty. By understanding its importance, calculating your saving target, and building your fund strategically, you lay the foundation for a secure financial future.

An emergency fund doesn't just prepare you for the unexpected—it liberates you from the anxieties of financial instability and empowers you to face life's challenges head-on. In the upcoming chapters, we'll delve into crafting your personalized saving plan, ensuring that your journey to financial resilience is both smart and manageable.

Chapter 2: Understanding Your Financial Landscape

Building a robust emergency fund is not unlike embarking on a journey to an unfamiliar destination. Before setting forth, it's crucial to lay out the map—a detailed understanding of your financial landscape.

Too often, individuals leap into the practice of saving without a comprehensive understanding of their current financial climate, leading to unnecessary stress and frustration. In this chapter, we will delve into the essential components of assessing your financial situation, enabling you to create a realistic and tailored emergency fund plan.

Budget: Your Financial Blueprint

Start by taking a thorough inventory of your income and expenses. This budget acts as your financial blueprint, guiding every decision. List all sources of income, from primary salaries to side gigs, taking care to account for all that flows into your household.

Next, catalog your monthly expenses meticulously. Divide them into two categories: fixed expenses (such as rent, utilities, and loan payments) and variable expenses (like groceries, entertainment, and dining out). This distinction will help identify areas where you can adjust spending in a meaningful way to free up funds for savings.

Creating a budget may seem straightforward, but one common pitfall is underestimating variable expenses or forgetting annual costs like insurance premiums or holiday spending.

For accuracy, review bank statements or use budgeting apps that track spending habits over time. Aim to strike a balance between realistic spending limits and necessary sacrifices.

Assessing Debt: Knowing the Burden

It's worth noting that For many, debt is a significant part of the financial landscape. Whether it's student loans, credit cards, or a mortgage, understanding the role debt plays in your financial situation is critical.

Make a comprehensive list of all debts, including interest rates and minimum payments. This exercise helps illuminate the financial burden debt places on your budget and lays the groundwork for prioritizing debt repayment alongside saving for your emergency fund.

You might wonder how to juggle debt repayment with saving, particularly if interest rates are high. While paying down debt is critical, it shouldn't come at the expense of having no emergency cushion, which could lead to more debt.

A balanced approach, such as allocating a portion of your budget to both debt repayment and emergency savings, can be wise. Evaluate if refinancing options could reduce your interest rates and free up more funds for saving.

Net Worth: Your Financial Health Snapshot

Your net worth provides a snapshot of your overall financial health.

It is calculated by subtracting liabilities (debts) from assets (savings, investments, real estate). A positive net worth indicates that you own more than you owe, whereas a negative net worth suggests the opposite.

To determine your net worth, start by listing your assets. Include checking and savings account balances, retirement accounts, investments, and any physical property owned, such as a home or car.

Next, sum up your liabilities, such as loan balances and credit card debt. By regularly calculating your net worth, you gain insight into your financial progress over time—a source of motivation when saving for an emergency fund may seem challenging.

Expense Tracking: Mindful Spending

Interestingly enough, Understanding your financial landscape isn't only about the bigger picture of budgets, debts, and net worth—it's also about the everyday spending habits that often go overlooked.

Mindful expense tracking can bring awareness to habitual spending that might be adjusted to improve savings.

Implement a system to track daily expenses. This could be as simple as a notebook or an app that categorizes spending to highlight patterns.

After a few months of diligent tracking, review your expenses critically. Are there subscriptions you no longer use? Is dining out draining more money than anticipated? Use these insights to make informed adjustments that support your emergency fund goals.

Setting Realistic Saving Goals

Interestingly enough, Armed with comprehensive knowledge from the above exercises, you can now set realistic saving goals.

Depending on the clarity gleaned from your financial landscape assessment, you might decide on saving a specific amount weekly or monthly. The beauty of understanding your financial situation deeply is that your goals align with your unique circumstances, making them more achievable.

While standard advice suggests an emergency fund covering three to six months of expenses, your target might vary based on personal circumstances, economic climate, or job stability.

Don't be discouraged if this goal seems daunting; remember, consistency in small contributions can compound over time into a considerable safety net.

Building Financial Resilience

A clear picture of your financial landscape not only aids in setting goals but also fosters resilience.

Understanding the ebb and flow of your finances prepares you to handle unforeseen challenges with less stress. As your circumstances evolve—such as a change in income or unexpected expenses—revisit your financial landscape regularly to adjust your strategy.

Consider unexpected scenarios, such as medical emergencies or sudden job loss, and how they might impact your financial plans.

Emergency funds should also account for these possibilities, reinforcing the need for adaptability in saving strategies.

Conclusion: Empowerment Through Knowledge

It's worth noting that Grasping the entirety of your financial landscape empowers you to make informed decisions about saving and spending.

Knowledge of your income, expenses, debts, net worth, and spending habits provides a solid foundation on which to construct a sustainable emergency fund. It's not about sacrificing too much but reallocating resources wisely to build a safety net.

The next steps involve strategic saving techniques, but without a comprehensive understanding of your financial situation, such strategies would lack the personalization necessary for success.

As you progress in this journey, remember that the path to financial security is defined more by persistence and informed choices than by vast sacrifices. Through knowledge comes power—power to safeguard your future with confidence.

Chapter 3: Setting Realistic Savings Goals

Saving money is a skill, not just a reaction to financial uncertainty. It's like anything else—we start with a basic idea and refine it through experience.

In the realm of saving, the starting point often involves defining realistic savings goals, which serve as your roadmap toward financial stability. In this chapter, we will delve into techniques and ideas for setting attainable goals that won't cause unnecessary strain on your day-to-day life.

Understanding the Importance of Goal Setting in Savings

Believe it or not, Many people fail in their savings efforts because they don't designate clear targets. Imagine heading on a cross-country road trip without a map or GPS.

Sure, you might eventually make it to your destination, but not without unnecessary detours and frustrations. Similarly, having savings goals sets your direction, giving your financial journey a purpose.

1.

Motivational Anchor: Savings goals are motivating forces. They give your financial choices a sense of purpose, ensuring that the hard work you put into cutting expenses or increasing revenue channels doesn't go to waste.

2. **Measurement Tool**: Goals offer a means to gauge your progress.

Without them, financial changes are abstract and harder to track. With clear targets, you can readily observe how close you are to your desired financial destination.

Many people don't realize this, but 3.

Financial Security: Realistic goals are the backbone of financial security, enabling you to build a safety net that ensures you're prepared for unexpected expenses or life changes.

Identifying and Prioritizing Your Goals

Begin by listing what you want to achieve with your savings.

These targets should encompass both short-term and long-term objectives, such as buying a new computer, setting up a fund for emergencies, or preparing for retirement. Once you've listed your goals, it's crucial to prioritize them based on urgency and importance.

Short-Term vs. Long-Term Goals

Having a mix of short-term and long-term goals maximizes motivation and provides continuous satisfaction. Short-term goals are typically achievable within a year, making milestones like holiday savings, minor home repairs, or a small emergency fund ideal candidates.

Long-term goals, on the other hand, may include major life events such as buying a house, funding children's education, or retirement. Balancing both categories will ensure steady progress.

Example of Short-Term Goal

- **Objective**: Save $500 for a new laptop within 12 months.

Let's not forget, - **Strategy**: Allocate $42 per month by reducing dining out and entertainment expenditures.

Example of Long-Term Goal

- **Objective**: Accumulate $10,000 for a rainy day in 5 years.

- **Strategy**: Contribute $167 monthly, potentially complemented by investing in mutual funds or bonds to benefit from growth over time.

Setting SMART Goals

The SMART criteria provide a framework for crafting your savings goals. Here's how to apply them:

1. **Specific**: Clearly define what you aim to accomplish.

- **Example**: "Save for a laptop" becomes "Save $1200 for a new laptop."

2. **Measurable**: Include exact figures and set periodic checkpoints.

- **Example**: Monitor your progress to ensure you save $100 monthly.

3. **Achievable**: Ensure your goals are within your reach based on your income and expenses.

- **Example**: If $100 monthly is challenging, reduce your goal or extend the timeline.

4. **Relevant**: Align goals with your broader life priorities.

- **Example**: Ensure your savings target complements larger ambitions, like owning a home or paying off debt.

5. **Time-Bound**: Set a realistic deadline to maintain motivation.

- **Example**: Establish a six-month timeline for accumulating the down payment for a car.

Breaking Down Your Goals

Interestingly enough, Large financial goals can be overwhelming, but they become more manageable when broken into smaller, digestible parts.

If your goal is to save $10,000 in three years, consider breaking it into smaller sums, such as $3,333 per year or $278 per month. This simplifies the process, enabling you to track monthly progress.

Evaluating Your Financial Situation

To ensure your goals are feasible, conduct a detailed assessment of your financial landscape.

This means evaluating your income, understanding your spending habits, and identifying areas for potential saving. Consider using a budgeting tool or app that categorizes your expenses and highlights discretionary spending opportunities.

Adjust and Reassess

Setting goals is not a one-time task but an evolving process. Life circumstances change, which means your savings goals might need to be adjusted.

At regular intervals, review and tweak these goals if necessary. Whenever possible, aim to enhance your contributions slightly with pay raises or reductions in other expenses.

Leveraging Tools and Resources

As strange as it sounds, In today's digital age, various online tools can make goal-setting simpler and more effective.

Many personal finance apps allow you to earmark savings for specific goals, providing visual cues to track your progress. Enabling automatic savings transfers to dedicated accounts can also facilitate disciplined saving practices.

The Role of an Accountability Partner

Pairing with a savings partner or accountability partner can enhance motivation.

Sharing your goals with someone who will check in with you periodically can create a sense of shared mission. This partnership creates a support system, offering encouragement and constructive feedback to maintain your course.

Conclusion

Setting realistic savings goals is an essential step in achieving financial security without undue sacrifice.

Through careful prioritization, clear articulation using SMART criteria, and the use of financial tools, your savings goals will guide you to a more stable financial future. Whether you're alleviating short-term financial pressure or ensuring long-term prosperity, sound savings goals will serve as valuable guideposts on your journey to financial well-being.

Chapter 4: Crafting Your Personalized Savings Plan

In the journey towards building a robust emergency fund, the pivotal step is crafting a savings plan that resonates with your personal financial circumstances and life goals.

While generic advice on saving can be a good starting point, a one-size-fits-all solution rarely captures the nuances of individual financial situations. In this chapter, we will delve into how you can formulate a savings strategy that is not just effective but also sustainable over the long term.

Understand Your Financial Landscape

Many people don't realize this, but Before jumping into a savings plan, it's crucial to have a clear picture of your current financial situation. Start by tracking your income streams and expenses.

There are numerous apps and tools available to simplify this process by automatically categorizing your spending. However, if you're inclined towards a more hands-on approach, a spreadsheet can be equally effective. The goal here is to understand where your money goes every month and identify areas where you may be able to cut back.

Moreover, categorize your expenses into fixed and variable expenses. Fixed expenses are those that don't change from month to month, such as rent or mortgage payments, insurance premiums, and utilities.

Variable expenses, on the other hand, can fluctuate and include groceries, dining out, and entertainment. Recognizing these distinctions will help you identify where you have flexibility to adjust your spending.

Define Your Savings Goals

It's worth noting that With a clear understanding of your financial landscape, the next step is to set tangible savings goals. Determine how much you want to save and the timeline for achieving this target.

Conventional wisdom suggests having three to six months' worth of living expenses in an emergency fund. However, your situation may require you to adjust this baseline. Consider your job security, the stability of your income, and any foreseeable financial obligations.

Once these considerations are assessed, write down specific, measurable goals.

Instead of a vague goal like "save for emergencies," specify something like "save $6,000 over the next 18 months. " This specificity not only makes your goal seem more real but also allows you to track progress and make adjustments when necessary.

Establish Your Budget

Many people don't realize this, but Creating a budget is where the theoretical aspects of saving meet practical application. Begin by identifying your necessary expenses—those that you need for survival and to maintain a certain standard of living.

This includes housing, utilities, groceries, healthcare, minimum debt payments, and basic transportation. Calculate these essentials to understand the minimum amount you need each month.

Next, prioritize your discretionary spending—the expenses that are not necessary but contribute to your quality of life, such as eating out, entertainment, and hobbies. This is where you'll find potential savings without resorting to extreme frugality.

It's often useful to set a budgetary limit on discretionary spending based on your unique priorities. For instance, if dining out is an important social activity, allocate more to that area but consider cutting back on other discretionary spending that's less important to you.

After accounting for essential and discretionary spending, allocate a portion of your remaining income to savings.

A popular approach is the 50/30/20 rule, where 50% of your income covers needs, 30% is for wants, and 20% goes to savings. However, feel free to adjust these percentages to suit your financial goals and lifestyle.

Implement Saving Strategies

Now that you have a budget in place, it's time to adopt methods that make saving easier and more consistent. One effective strategy is to automate your savings.

Set up automatic transfers from your checking to your savings account each payday. This ensures saving becomes a regular habit rather than an afterthought.

Another useful strategy is to earmark any windfalls—like tax refunds or bonuses—entirely or partially for your emergency fund.

This approach can accelerate your savings progress significantly without affecting your day-to-day finances.

I've seen this happen before: For those months when unexpected expenses crop up, having buffer categories in your budget can be beneficial.

These are allocations for contingencies, allowing you to manage unforeseen costs without dipping into your savings.

Moreover, engage in periodic reviews of your savings plan.

Financial circumstances can change, sometimes rather unexpectedly. An annual review—or more frequently if there are significant changes in your life—helps keep your plan in alignment with your goals.

Practical Tips for Staying On Track

In real life, Maintaining motivation over time is one of the more challenging aspects of a savings plan.

To keep the momentum going, consider tracking your progress visually. Whether through spreadsheets, apps, or even a simple chart on the wall, seeing your growth can encourage continued commitment.

Furthermore, reward yourself for meeting milestones.

The rewards don't have to be extravagant—perhaps a nice meal out or a small treat—but having something to look forward to makes the saving process less monotonous.

Finally, engage with a supportive community.

Whether it's online forums, social media groups, or personal friends and family, sharing your goals and achievements can provide encouragement and new ideas to stay on track.

Tailoring to Life Changes

Life is dynamic, and your savings plan should be flexible enough to accommodate changes. Significant life events—such as getting married, having children, or changing careers—can drastically affect your financial outlook.

Be prepared to revisit and adjust your savings plan during these transitions. This might mean increasing your savings rate, diversifying your investments, or reprioritizing your financial goals altogether.

Conclusion

Crafting a personalized savings plan is not about imposing strict limitations, but about creating a sustainable path toward financial security. By understanding your financial landscape, setting clear goals, establishing a realistic budget, and implementing smart saving strategies, you build a robust financial foundation.

Remember, the aim is to save smart without living in deprivation. With a tailored plan in place, you're not only prepared for future uncertainties but also empowered to pursue a financially stable and fulfilling life.

Chapter 5: Budgeting Basics: Building a Strong Foundation

In any sensible journey towards financial independence, establishing a strong foundation through budgeting is paramount.

Budgeting isn't about holding onto every penny; instead, it's about knowing where your money goes and ensuring it aligns with your goals, such as building an emergency fund. This chapter delves into the building blocks of creating a solid budget that can withstand life's uncertainties without forcing significant sacrifices.

Understanding Your Income

At first glance, The first step in budgeting is having a clear picture of your total income. For most people, this includes their salary or wages, but it could also encompass other earnings such as rental income, side hustles, dividends, or alimony.

It's essential to calculate your net income, which is the amount you actually take home after taxes and deductions. This figure is the cornerstone of your budget since it represents the real money available for your expenses and savings.

To avoid underestimating or overestimating your earnings, consider seasonal changes in your income.

If you have a job that offers bonuses, works on commission, or fluctuates seasonally, base your budget on your lowest expected monthly income to build a cushion for leaner months.

Tracking Expenses

Once you have a firm grasp on your income, the next phase is to track how you spend your money.

This step might require patience and diligence, as keeping tabs on all expenditures can be eye-opening. For this, you can use a budgeting app, a spreadsheet, or even a pen and paper—the key is consistency.

Categories of Expenses:

1. **Fixed Expenses:** These are regular, unchanging payments such as rent or mortgage, loan payments, insurance premiums, and subscriptions.

I've seen this happen before: 2. **Variable Expenses:** These include utilities, groceries, transportation, and any cost that fluctuates month to month.

3. **Discretionary Expenses:** This category covers non-essential spending, such as entertainment, dining out, and hobbies.

4.

Occasional Expenses: Often overlooked, these are sporadic expenses like car maintenance, medical bills, or gifts. Forecasting these costs by setting aside a small amount monthly can prevent budget derailment.

Once categorized, analyze your past three months of spending to identify patterns and areas that require adjustment.

Notice where you're overspending and consider cutting back or finding alternatives.

Setting Budget Goals

With a clear understanding of your income and expenses, you can start setting realistic goals. Begin by prioritizing your essential expenses and financial responsibilities.

Then allocate funds toward your savings goals, including your emergency fund. A standard guideline suggests saving at least 20% of your income, but this might vary based on individual circumstances and obligations.

SMART Goals: Ensure your savings goals are Specific, Measurable, Achievable, Relevant, and Time-bound.

For instance, rather than vaguely stating, "I want to save money," specify, "I will save $500 monthly for six months to reach a $3,000 emergency fund. ".

Creating and Managing the Budget

A zero-sum budget is one effective method, where every dollar has a purpose, either toward expenses, savings, or investing.

By allocating exactly what you earn, you not only cover all necessary expenses but also strategically build savings into the framework.

Steps to Create a Budget:

1. **List Income Sources:** Clearly indicate all potential sources of income.

2. **Detail All Expenses:** Break down your spending using the categories defined above.

In real life, 3.

Calculate the Difference: Subtract total expenses (and savings goals) from your income. The aim is to reach zero, meaning each penny is accounted for.

4.

Adjust Accordingly: If your expenses surpass your income, identify areas to cut back or rethink how to increase your income. If you have surplus cash, consider directing more toward your emergency fund or paying down debt.

Tools for Success

Harness budgeting tools and apps that can make this process more accessible and fun.

Applications like YNAB (You Need A Budget), Mint, or Goodbudget provide structure and real-time tracking, making adjusting your strategy straightforward.

Additionally, setting up direct deposits into savings accounts can foster discipline, ensuring commitment to saving rather than spending.

Regular Reviewing

I've seen this happen before: Budgeting is not a set-it-and-forget-it task.

Economic conditions, changes in circumstance, or shifts in personal priorities necessitate periodic budget reviews. Develop a habit of checking your budget monthly, if not more frequently, and make necessary tweaks to ensure alignment with your goals.

Overcoming Budgeting Challenges

Budgeting might introduce challenges, such as irregular income, unforeseen expenses, and the temptation to overspend.

Build buffer amounts into your categories to cushion unexpected costs. Furthermore, an accountability partner, perhaps a spouse or friend, can offer support and encouragement in adhering to your budget.

Conclusion

Budgeting forms the essential foundation of financial well-being and is central to establishing a robust emergency fund. It's not merely about restricting spending but realigning financial habits to reflect your aspirations.

As you embark or continue on this budgeting journey, remember that flexibility, vigilance, and adaptation are key. By building a strong budgetary foundation, you empower yourself against surprises and cultivate a greater sense of financial independence. This chapter's insights and practical steps offer an essential cornerstone in your larger financial strategy, ultimately enriching your path to a secure future.

Chapter 6: Identifying Non-Essential Expenses

Creating an emergency fund is a crucial step to ensuring financial stability and peace of mind. The journey begins with gaining a clear understanding of your financial landscape, which includes distinguishing between essential and non-essential expenses.

Knowing the difference can be the key to unlocking hidden funds for your savings without the stress of feeling like you're giving up too much. In this chapter, we will explore practical steps to identify non-essential expenses in your life, so you can redirect those dollars into your emergency fund, fostering a robust financial safety net.

Understanding Needs vs. Wants

To be honest, Before diving into identifying non-essential expenses, it's essential to establish a clear distinction between needs and wants. Essentials are those expenses required for basic living, such as housing, utilities, groceries, healthcare, and transportation.

These are the costs that keep your everyday life functioning and healthy. Non-essential expenses, on the other hand, are your wants—items and services that enhance your lifestyle but which you can live without if necessary.

A simple way to start categorizing your expenses is by creating a list.

Begin by listing all your monthly expenses, categorizing each one as either a 'need' or a 'want. ' This straightforward exercise allows you to visually separate the two and start evaluating where modifications can be made.

Keeping Track of Your Spending

Many people don't realize this, but A crucial tool in identifying non-essential expenses is tracking your expenditure diligently.

This approach provides concrete insight into where your money is going and assists in pinpointing areas where you might be overspending. Several methods can help you keep track of your spending:.

- **Use Technology:** Leverage budgeting apps or financial software that connects with your bank accounts and categorizes your transactions automatically.

These platforms can provide a monthly snapshot of your spending, highlighting areas of concern.

- **Manual Tracking:** If you prefer a hands-on approach, consider maintaining a spending journal.

Physically writing down each expenditure can increase mindfulness about how much you're spending and on what.

It's worth noting that - **Bank Statements:** Regularly review your bank and credit card statements to spot recurring non-essential expenses you might overlook.

Conducting a Spending Audit

After compiling a detailed record of your expenses, conduct a spending audit. This is an in-depth look at where your money has gone over the past three to six months.

Pay attention to patterns and categorize each expense once more, using your newfound data to reassess the needs versus wants distinction. During this audit, consider the following:.

- **Subscriptions and Memberships:** Are you utilizing all your subscriptions, such as streaming services, gym memberships, and magazine subscriptions? If not, canceling underused services can free up significant funds each month.

- **Dining Out:** Analyze the frequency and cost of eating out, including takeaways and coffee runs.

Preparing meals at home or reducing the number of dining occasions can make a notable impact on your budget.

- **Entertainment and Leisure:** Be honest about how much you spend on non-essential leisure activities and look for areas to cut back.

Local, low-cost alternatives may provide similar enjoyment with a much smaller price tag.

Prioritizing and Setting Limits

Once you have successfully identified non-essential expenses, the next step is to prioritize those that bring the most value and set limits on them.

This can help you maintain a balanced lifestyle without feeling deprived. Each individual has different priorities, so consider what truly enriches your life versus what might be habitual, convenience-based, or impulse-driven.

- **Set a Monthly Fun Budget:** Establish a reasonable amount you can spend on discretionary fun expenses each month.

Stick to this limit proudly, knowing that every dollar saved is a dollar closer to your future security.

Interestingly enough, - **Consider Impact vs. Expense:** Evaluate the impact of each non-essential expense.

For example, a monthly book club fee might be inexpensive but enriches your life through social interaction and intellectual stimulation. Meanwhile, spending on designer clothes might not have the same personal significance.

Cultivating Mindful Spending Habits

Identifying non-essential expenses is not just a one-time task but a lifelong practice.

Cultivating mindful spending habits ensures you remain aware of your financial decisions and their consequences. Here are some strategies to develop these habits:.

Let's not forget, - **Pause Before Purchasing:** Implement a 24- or 48-hour rule before making non-essential purchases.

This time buffer allows you to reconsider your needs and prevents impulse buying.

- **Reflect on Your Purchases:** Regularly reflect on your recent purchases.

Ask yourself if they brought you joy or value and how they might impact your financial goals.

- **Revisit and Revise:** Life circumstances change, and so will your definition of essential versus non-essential. Periodically revisit and adjust your budget accordingly.

The Long-Term Benefits

By honing in on your non-essential expenses and adjusting your lifestyle accordingly, you'll find surplus money to add to your emergency fund without the need for drastic lifestyle changes.

The process reinforces mindful spending habits and builds a foundation for financial resilience, empowering you to handle unexpected expenses with confidence and grace.

With practice, identifying non-essential expenses becomes intuitive, fostering financial clarity and discipline.

Remember that every journey is unique. Be kind to yourself, stay committed to your goals, and celebrate the progress toward a stronger financial future.

Chapter 7: Smart Cutbacks Without Feeling Deprived

Creating an emergency fund is like building a safety net that will catch you in times of financial uncertainty. However, the task of amassing such savings frequently implies that you must tighten your belt and live a life of austerity to make it happen.

As daunting as that might sound, the good news is that you can make intelligent cutbacks without feeling deprived or sacrificing your quality of life. The key lies in strategic changes that benefit your budget while allowing you to enjoy everyday life. Here's how you do it.

Understanding Needs vs. Wants

The first step is to clearly differentiate between needs and wants. Needs are essentials required to maintain a basic standard of living—think food, shelter, utilities, and healthcare. Wants, on the other hand, are things that add pleasure or comfort but are not essential.

When evaluating cutbacks, focus on scaling down the wants, without touching the needs. Take a closer look at your spendings. Are you eating out three times a week? Is every weekend a shopping spree? By distinguishing needs from wants, you'll find areas ripe for smart cutbacks.

Step One: Reset Your Subscriptions

Today, it's easy to subscribe to a multitude of services, from streaming platforms to monthly magazine subscriptions. Start by reviewing all your subscriptions.

Are there any that you are barely using or that duplicate others? For instance, if you're subscribed to multiple TV or music streaming services, consider keeping only the one you use the most. Evaluate magazine or news subscriptions critically—many of these can be read online for free or borrowed from a library. Restricting your subscriptions to the essentials can free up significant amounts of money annually.

Step Two: Home Cooking is Key

Eating out or ordering takeout regularly can quickly drain your finances. Cooking at home is one of the smartest cutbacks that can drastically reduce expenses without compromising on quality of life.

Start by planning your meals for the week around sales or discounts at your local grocery store, which helps you to optimize savings further. Additionally, cooking at home allows for healthier meal choices and can be a creative activity to de-stress. Perhaps try new recipes that replicate your favorite restaurant dishes at a fraction of the cost.

Step Three: Optimize Utility Usage

It's worth noting that While utility bills fall under the needs category, optimizing their usage is an excellent way to reduce expenses smartly. Implementing small changes such as turning off lights in unoccupied rooms, unplugging devices when not in use, and taking shorter showers can collectively make a big difference.

Investing in energy-efficient appliances or using a programmable thermostat might also save money in the long run. Get the entire family involved by making a game out of conserving electricity or water, transforming this into a shared goal rather than a deprivation.

Step Four: Revisit Your Transportation Habits

Transportation is a necessity, but finding economical methods of getting from point A to B can lead to valuable savings. If you're a car owner, look into carpooling, ridesharing, or using public transportation, which can sometimes be more cost-effective.

If your destination is nearby, consider biking or walking for added health benefits. Regularly servicing your car improves fuel efficiency, saving money on gas. By strategically altering how you view transportation, you can cut back sensibly without losing convenience.

Step Five: Embrace the Second-Hand Economy

We often equate the new with the best, but second-hand goods can often meet your requirements at much lower prices. Whether it's clothes, furniture, electronics, or books, buying second-hand can offer significant monetary relief.

Explore thrift stores, online marketplaces, or local garage sales. Often, you'll find items in excellent condition for a fraction of their original cost. By shifting your mindset to embrace second-hand shopping, you'll ease a substantial strain from your expenses.

Step Six: Relive Experiences Over Material Goods

Many people don't realize this, but When planning how to spend your discretionary income, focus on experiences rather than material acquisitions. People often find greater satisfaction from experiences such as attending a community event, visiting a park, or engaging in a hobby.

These experiences usually cost far less than purchasing new items and contribute more meaningfully to your well-being and happiness. Thus, you make room for living a richer life in terms of experiences while staying financially disciplined.

Step Seven: Streamline Your Debt

While not technically a cutback, accelerating debt repayment can dramatically improve your financial health. Small adjustments, such as limiting new borrowing and redirecting even a small portion of discretionary spending to pay down high-interest debt faster, will free up more funds.

You can then divert this into building your emergency fund. Consider prioritizing high-interest debts or consolidating multiple loans for lower interest rates to manage repayments more effectively. Identifying unnecessary debt-related expenses is an action plan that can stop wastage effortlessly.

Observing the Long Term Benefits

It's crucial to continually review expenditures against savings, not only for building an emergency fund but fostering a sustainable financial future.

An annual analysis of your spending habits will reveal if you're gradually slipping back into old habits, and provide the motivation to recommit to smart cutbacks.

Remember, the goal of cutbacks is not to create an environment of deprivation. Instead, it's about making smart financial choices that keep your present lifestyle pleasant while securing your financial future.

Integrating these strategies into your life can help you save effectively without feeling like you're missing out. By implementing these strategies, you're not only contributing to your emergency fund but also embracing a more thoughtful, strategic approach to everyday expenditures. This journey isn't about restriction—it's about empowerment and making choices that support your life goals for the long haul.

I've seen this happen before: As you navigate this transformative process, remember that flexibility is your ally. Not every cutback will work for everyone in the same way.

Adjust based on what makes the most sense for your financial picture and personal lifestyle. Integrating smart cutbacks into your daily routine is less daunting when they seamlessly align with your life's priorities and bring you peace of mind alongside fiscal stability.

Chapter 8: Mastering the Art of Mindful Spending

In our fast-paced, consumer-driven world, mastering the art of mindful spending is an essential skill for anyone striving to build a solid emergency fund without sacrificing their quality of life.

The term "mindful spending" refers to making intentional decisions about where and how you spend your money, ensuring that your expenditures align with your values and long-term financial goals. By honing this skill, you can significantly enhance your financial well-being while still enjoying the things that truly matter to you.

Understanding Your Spending Habits

It's worth noting that The first step in mastering mindful spending is understanding your current spending habits. Begin by tracking your expenses for an entire month.

Use a simple spreadsheet, a budgeting app, or even a good old-fashioned notebook to jot down every penny you spend. While this might seem tedious, the insights you gain are invaluable. You'll spot patterns and identify areas where you might be overspending.

Examine your expenses and categorize them into needs and wants. Needs include essentials like housing, utilities, groceries, and transportation.

Wants, on the other hand, encompass non-essential items like dining out, entertainment, and luxury purchases. Be honest with yourself about what constitutes a need versus a want.

Cultivating Awareness and Reflection

Many people don't realize this, but Mindful spending requires you to be present and aware each time you make a purchase.

Before reaching for your wallet, pause and reflect. Ask yourself a series of questions: Why am I buying this? Do I need it, or do I want it? Does this purchase align with my values and financial goals? Could this money be better spent elsewhere, such as adding to my emergency fund?.

This practice encourages you to think critically about your spending decisions and to avoid impulse buys that can derail your savings efforts.

Over time, you will likely find that the act of pausing and reflecting becomes second nature, fostering a more disciplined approach to spending.

Setting Intentional Financial Goals

Mindful spending is closely linked to goal setting. By defining clear financial goals, you create a roadmap that guides your spending decisions.

Start by setting short-term, medium-term, and long-term goals. Short-term goals might include reducing your monthly dining-out budget, while medium-term goals could involve saving for a vacation or a major purchase. Long-term goals often focus on retirement savings or achieving financial independence.

Once you establish these goals, rank them by priority and attach a timeline to each. These goals should not only be specific but also achievable.

For example, rather than setting a vague goal like "save more money," specify the amount you plan to save each month. Revisit and adjust your goals as your financial situation and priorities evolve.

Practicing Delayed Gratification

At first glance, One of the most powerful techniques in mindful spending is practicing delayed gratification. This involves resisting the urge to make an immediate purchase to achieve a longer-term objective.

When you see something you'd like to buy, wait 24 hours before making a decision. This waiting period gives you time to evaluate whether the purchase is truly necessary, or if it's simply a fleeting desire.

Delayed gratification not only protects your wallet but also helps you develop greater self-control and discipline.

It shifts the focus from impulsive decisions to thoughtful, deliberate ones that serve your larger financial goals.

Embracing Minimalism and Simplicity

To be honest, The principles of minimalism and simplicity can significantly enhance your journey toward mindful spending.

Minimalism encourages you to prioritize experiences and relationships over material possessions. By adopting a minimalist mindset, you naturally reduce the desire for unnecessary items, allowing you to allocate more resources toward building an emergency fund.

Simplicity involves paring down your life to its essentials, minimizing clutter, and focusing on what truly adds value.

As you simplify your lifestyle, you gain clarity on what matters most, making it easier to align your spending with your values.

The Power of Gratitude and Contentment

I've seen this happen before: Gratitude and contentment are essential components of mindful spending.

By cultivating an attitude of gratitude, you shift your focus from what you lack to what you already have. This perspective reduces the urge to seek happiness through material possessions and fosters a sense of contentment with your current financial state.

Make it a habit to reflect on the positives in your life regularly.

Keep a gratitude journal where you note down things you appreciate, both big and small. This practice not only enhances your overall well-being but also reinforces the realization that contentment is not tied to acquiring more things.

Seeking Quality Over Quantity

Believe it or not, Another aspect of mindful spending is prioritizing quality over quantity.

While it may be tempting to buy cheaper, lower-quality items, investing in fewer, high-quality products can provide better value in the long run. Quality items tend to last longer and often come with warranties or support, which can save you money on replacements or repairs.

Whether it's clothing, electronics, or household items, opting for quality ensures you're making a wise investment in your needs and future savings.

Being Conscious of Marketing and Consumer Traps

Understanding the strategies employed by marketers can help you navigate consumer traps designed to entice you into spending.

Be cautious of sales, discounts, and limited-time promotions, which often create a sense of urgency and fear of missing out. While these tactics can provide genuine savings, approach them with skepticism and ensure they align with your financial goals.

Furthermore, avoid succumbing to lifestyle inflation, which occurs when increased income leads to increased spending.

Instead of upgrading your lifestyle with every pay rise, consider investing the extra money into your savings, particularly your emergency fund.

Creating Space for Generosity and Giving

Let's not forget, Finally, as you adopt a mindful approach to spending, create space in your budget for generosity and giving.

The act of giving, whether it's to charity, community initiatives, or helping others in need, can bring immense satisfaction and foster a sense of purpose.

Incorporating giving into your financial plan doesn't mean you have to compromise on your savings goals.

By being intentional with your spending, you can identify areas where you can cut back, allowing you to allocate resources to causes you believe in.

Conclusion

In real life, Mastering the art of mindful spending is a skill that evolves with practice and dedication.

It allows you to make intentional choices that reflect your values and financial objectives, minimizing unnecessary stress and maximizing the joy derived from aligning with what matters most. By integrating these practices into your daily life, you can contribute more effectively to your emergency fund, ensuring financial security without sacrificing the essence of what makes life fulfilling.

Chapter 9: Maximizing Income: Side Hustles and Opportunities

In an era where life's financial demands are a consistent reality, finding ways to maximize income is an increasingly vital skill.

While saving diligently and sticking to a budget can significantly improve your financial situation, enhancing your income through side hustles can expedite the journey toward a robust emergency fund. This chapter explores the world of side hustles and additional opportunities, offering practical guidance on identifying suitable options and effectively managing this supplementary income.

The Case for Side Hustles

Interestingly enough, A side hustle is often the bridge between financial insufficiency and security. By generating extra income, not only do you enhance your capacity to save, but you also mitigate the risks posed by potential job loss or unexpected expenses.

With the rising costs of living, many people find that a single source of income falls short of meeting all financial needs and aspirations. Side hustles provide a flexible solution—allowing you to balance additional work with your primary job and personal life.

Identifying the Right Side Hustle

The ideal side hustle leverages your existing skills, interests, and available time. Here are steps to identify a side hustle that fits your lifestyle:

1.

Skill Inventory: Begin with a self-assessment of your skills and talents. Are you good at graphic design, writing, tutoring, or web development? Perhaps you have organizational skills or love pets? Define what you're good at and enjoy.

2.

Research Opportunities: Once you have a list of skills, research potential opportunities where these can be monetized. The gig economy provides myriad platforms like Upwork, Fiverr, and Etsy, offering work in categories from freelance writing to handmade crafts.

3.

Time Management: Evaluate how much time you can realistically commit to a side hustle without affecting your primary job or personal life. The consistency of effort often matters more than the total hours spent.

It's worth noting that 4. **Market Demand:** Some side hustles are more lucrative than others due to market demand.

Investigate the demand for your skills. High-demand skills generally offer better pay and more job security.

5.

Passion and Enjoyment: Your side hustle should ideally be something you enjoy, so it doesn't feel burdensome. Doing something you love can lead to greater success and happiness, improving both the quality of your work and personal satisfaction.

Popular Side Hustles to Consider

At first glance, Here are several popular and practical side hustle opportunities worth considering:

- **Freelancing:** Platforms like Upwork and Freelancer allow you to offer your skills—be it writing, design, programming, or marketing—to a global client base.

- **Online Tutoring:** If you are knowledgeable in a subject area, platforms such as VIPKid or Chegg Tutors offer avenues for teaching students worldwide.

As strange as it sounds, - **E-Commerce:** Consider selling handmade products on Etsy or used items on eBay or Poshmark.

Alternatively, drop shipping with platforms like Shopify allows you to create custom e-commerce stores.

- **Gig Economy Jobs:** Companies like Uber, Lyft, DoorDash, and Instacart provide flexible, on-demand work that can be tailored around your schedule.

- **Real Estate and Renting:** If you have unused space, renting it through Airbnb can be lucrative.

It requires initial setup efforts but can perform well with the right location and marketing.

In real life, - **Content Creation:** Blogging, YouTube, or podcasting can eventually generate income through advertising, sponsorship, and merchandise, although they may require significant upfront effort.

Managing Your Side Hustle Earnings

Increasing your income is just one part of the financial empowerment equation. Equally important is managing this additional income effectively:

Many people don't realize this, but - **Budget Allocation:** Decide in advance how you will allocate your side hustle earnings.

Consider earmarking a percentage exclusively for your emergency fund.

- **Track Your Earnings:** Keep meticulous records of your income and expenses related to your side hustle.

Not only is this crucial for tax purposes, but it also helps in evaluating the sustainability and profitability of your effort.

- **Tax Considerations:** Understand the tax implications of your side hustle.

Use software like QuickBooks Self-Employed or consult a tax professional to ensure you are filing correctly and taking advantage of any deductible expenses.

Let's not forget, - **Reinvesting Earnings:** Consider reinvesting a portion of your side hustle earnings into your business.

Whether it's purchasing better tools or taking courses to enhance your skills, reinvestment can lead to greater efficiency and earnings down the line.

Balancing Act: Avoiding Burnout

While the allure of extra income is tempting, balancing a side hustle along with other life responsibilities is critical:

Interestingly enough, - **Set Limits:** Establish clear boundaries around your side hustle to prevent it from overtaking your primary job or family time.

Designate specific hours for your side hustle work.

- **Regular Evaluation:** Periodically assess whether the side hustle still aligns with your goals and make changes if necessary.

As your life circumstances change, so too should your side hustle strategy.

- **Self-Care:** Prioritize well-being by ensuring that your schedule includes downtime. Regular breaks and the freedom to disconnect are important for long-term productivity and happiness.

Conclusion

Side hustles offer a practical path to enhancing your income without the need for major lifestyle sacrifices. By selecting opportunities that align with your skills and interests, managing your earnings wisely, and maintaining a careful balance, you can significantly speed up your progress toward financial security.

The strategic use of side hustles not only diversifies your income streams but also builds a diligent work ethic and entrepreneurial mindset that can reap benefits beyond your emergency fund goals. In an increasingly dynamic economic landscape, mastering the art of the side hustle is an invaluable component of smart financial planning.

Chapter 10: Automating Your Savings for Consistency

One of the most significant challenges in building an emergency fund is ensuring regular contributions. Life tends to throw many financial obligations our way, from unexpected expenses to tempting purchases.

However, one of the smartest strategies you can employ to ensure you consistently save is to automate your savings. Automation can transform the process from one that requires your constant attention and discipline to one that occurs seamlessly in the background of your daily life. In this chapter, we'll explore how to effectively automate your savings, ensuring that you're consistently working towards your emergency fund goal without having to think about it all the time.

Understanding the Benefits of Automation

To be honest, Automation is essentially about setting and forgetting—creating a financial system that manages itself. By automating your savings, you achieve the following benefits:

1. **Consistency**: Automated savings mean that you are consistently putting money towards your emergency fund, removing the temptation to use that money elsewhere.

2. **Discipline Without Effort**: You remove the human element of procrastination and impulsive spending because your savings are deducted automatically.

Believe it or not, 3.

Time-Saving: Automation frees up time and mental energy, allowing you to focus on other essential aspects of your financial life without constantly tracking your contributions.

4. **Reduced Anxiety**: Knowing that your savings are being handled regularly can provide peace of mind and reduce the stress associated with financial planning.

Steps to Automate Your Savings

In real life, To harness the power of automation, follow these practical steps:

1. Decide Your Savings Amount

Before you automate, decide how much money you can comfortably save each month for your emergency fund.

Consider your income, expenses, and overall budget to determine a realistic amount. Remember, the key is to start with a manageable sum, and as your financial situation improves, you can increase this amount.

2. Choose the Right Account

Select a separate savings account specifically for your emergency fund.

Ensure it offers easy access in times of emergency, yet isn't linked to your checking account to avoid the temptation of frequent withdrawals. Look for a high-yield savings account to maximize your interest earnings.

3. Set Up Automatic Transfers

As strange as it sounds, Once you have your savings account ready, initiate automatic transfers from your checking account to your savings account.

Most banks allow you to set up recurring transfers on a schedule that suits you, such as bi-weekly or monthly. Typically, aligning this transfer with payday ensures you prioritize saving before spending.

4. Consider Employer Benefits

Some employers offer direct deposit allocation where your paycheck is split and sent to different accounts.

Check with your HR department to see if this option is available, allowing you to direct a portion of your income directly into your emergency fund.

5. Use Financial Apps and Tools

Take advantage of financial apps that facilitate automated saving.

Apps like Qapital, Digit, and Chime analyze spending habits, rounding up purchases to the nearest dollar, and transferring the difference to savings. They make saving automatic and often effortless.

Fine-Tuning Your Strategy

It's worth noting that Automating savings is not a "set it and forget it" task entirely. It requires occasional review:

1. **Regular Review**: Schedule a quarterly review of your savings goals. Check if your contribution amount needs adjusting based on changes in your financial situation.

2.

Automate Increases: As your income grows, increase your automated savings. Some bank platforms allow you to set up automatic annual increases to your savings, ensuring your emergency fund grows in line with your earnings.

Many people don't realize this, but 3.

Adjust for Life Changes: Major life changes—such as getting married, purchasing a home, or having children—can influence your financial situation. Reassess your savings levels to ensure they match any new financial commitments.

Avoiding Potential Pitfalls

While automation is powerful, be mindful of potential pitfalls:

I've seen this happen before: - **Overdraft Risks**: Ensure your checking account always has enough balance to cover the automated transfer, avoiding overdraft fees.

- **Complacency**: Automation is convenient but doesn't eliminate the need for vigilance. Regularly monitor your account for any erroneous transactions or changes in fees.

- **Unmonitored Growth**: While an emergency fund should be accessible, too much accumulated money in low-interest savings isn't optimal.

Once goals are achieved, keep excess funds working harder in other investment vehicles.

Conclusion

Automation is a powerful ally in your journey to building an effective emergency fund. It minimizes the effort, maximizes consistency, and ensures you remain on track towards your financial safety net goals.

Adopt automation to ease your savings process, but remain engaged enough to react as your financial landscape evolves. In doing so, you'll secure your peace of mind and enhance your ability to handle life's unforeseen financial challenges without sacrificing your day-to-day comfort. By automating your savings for consistency, you are laying down a foundation of financial resilience that will serve you well in the toughest of times.

Chapter 11: Banking Options: Choosing the Right Account

Creating an effective emergency fund is akin to building a house; a strong foundation is critical for safety and longevity.

Just as the foundation anchors a house, the right banking account choice anchors your emergency fund, ensuring it is accessible, secure, and growing. In this chapter, we'll explore various banking options, evaluating their advantages and disadvantages to empower you to make informed decisions tailored to your unique financial situation.

Understanding the Essentials

Before diving into the specific types of accounts, it's essential to understand what we seek in the ideal emergency fund account. The main criteria include:

1. **Liquidity**: The ability to quickly and easily access your money without penalties.

As strange as it sounds, 2. **Safety**: Your funds should be protected from undue risk, preserving your capital.

3. **Interest Rate**: An account that offers a competitive interest rate can mitigate inflation's erosive impact on purchasing power.

4. **Minimal Fees**: Accounts with low to no maintenance fees are preferable, ensuring more of your money stays with you.

With these criteria in mind, let's explore the various banking options available.

Traditional Savings Accounts

Traditional savings accounts are often the first port of call.

Widely offered by banks and credit unions, they provide a straightforward way to store cash. Here are the key benefits and drawbacks:.

- **Pros**: Highly liquid and generally insured up to a certain amount by federal protection (like FDIC in the U. S.

), these accounts are safe. They're accessible, with easy transfers between accounts and ATM withdrawals.

- **Cons**: The interest rates tend to be low, sometimes not keeping pace with inflation.

Some banks charge maintenance fees unless a minimum balance is maintained.

To maximize benefits, consider bank promotions; switching or opening new accounts during promotional periods can secure higher initial rates or waived fees.

High-Yield Savings Accounts (HYSAs)

High-yield savings accounts often reside with online banks rather than traditional brick-and-mortar institutions. Offering significantly higher interest rates, they can be particularly appealing.

- **Pros**: They offer much higher interest rates than traditional savings accounts, are usually fee-free, and still provide the same level of federal insurance.

- **Cons**: Slightly less approachable than standard savings accounts. The absence of physical branches means everything is done online, which might not suit everyone.

Ensure you check the account conditions carefully; some high yield accounts require a minimum balance to maintain the high interest rate, or the rate might only be introductory, dropping after a few months.

Money Market Accounts

Money Market Accounts (MMAs) combine features of savings and checking accounts. They provide attractive interest rates while allowing occasional access to funds beyond transfers.

- **Pros**: Competitive interest rates and the ability to write checks or use a debit card for limited transactions.

- **Cons**: MMAs often come with higher minimum balance requirements and may have fees if your balance dips below that threshold.

These accounts are ideal if you have a sizeable emergency fund already, as you can maximize interest benefits without worrying as much about the balance limitations.

Certificates of Deposit (CDs)

Certificates of Deposit are time-bound deposit accounts with committed terms ranging from months to years. They offer fixed interest but restrict access to funds.

- **Pros**: Higher interest rates, especially for longer terms, with federally insured security.

- **Cons**: Funds are locked for a specified term; early withdrawal incurs penalties, reducing liquidity.

Laddering CDs can offer a compromise between maximizing interest and maintaining accessibility.

Divide your emergency fund among several CDs with staggered maturity dates, ensuring regular access to a portion of your funds.

Let's not forget, #### Roth Individual Retirement Account (Roth IRA)

A Roth IRA isn't a conventional emergency fund account, yet, for some, it offers strategic advantages. Contributions—not earnings—can be withdrawn without taxes or penalties.

- **Pros**: Tax-free growth and withdrawals, flexible contribution use, with the added benefit of retirement savings.

- **Cons**: Withdrawals should primarily be considered a last resort; ideally, Roth IRAs should remain undisturbed for future retirement income.

Due diligence is crucial; ensure any withdrawals are strictly from contributions to avoid taxes and penalties on earnings.

Consider Credit Union Options

Credit unions are member-owned financial cooperatives known for favorable rates and lower fees.

As non-profits focused on member satisfaction rather than profits, they often present attractive savings alternatives.

- **Pros**: Better interest rates and lower fees, coupled with a community-focused approach.

- **Cons**: Membership eligibility can be restricted based on geographical location, industry, or other qualifying factors.

Credit unions might require a small deposit to open an account, but this initial step could open doors to other financial benefits.

Evaluating Online Banking

Online-only banks offer compelling features that frequently eclipse traditional institutions, primarily due to reduced overhead costs that translate into better rates and lower fees for consumers.

Evaluate online banks based on user experience, customer service options, and digital security standards.

Ensure the bank has a reputable history and robust measures in place to protect your financial data.

Final Thoughts

Choosing the right account for your emergency fund doesn't need to be overwhelming. Assess your financial habits, risk tolerance, and accessibility needs to align with potential account benefits.

It's critical to remember that what works for one individual might not suit another. Your life circumstances, your habits, and even your financial goals will dictate the best option for you.

Above all, remain zealous in your dedication to maintaining and growing your emergency fund.

With the right account infrastructure, you pave the way for greater financial resilience, ensuring unforeseen events are endured with confidence rather than consternation.

Chapter 12: The Power of Compound Interest

Welcome to a pivotal chapter in your journey towards financial resilience—one that introduces you to the transformative concept of compound interest. Often described as the eighth wonder of the world, compound interest is a potent financial tool that can significantly accelerate the growth of your emergency fund.

Yet, its power can be elusive to those who aren't familiar with how it functions. This chapter seeks to demystify compound interest and illustrate the strategic advantage it offers in building and maintaining your financial safety net.

Understanding Compound Interest

At its core, compound interest is the interest you earn on both the initial principal amount and on the accumulated interest of previous periods.

Unlike simple interest, which is calculated only on the principal amount, compound interest exponentially enhances your savings by reinvesting the earned interest back into your principal balance. This creates a snowball effect, where the interest of one period earns interest in subsequent periods.

To better understand this concept, imagine you have $1,000 in a savings account with an annual interest rate of 5% that compounds annually. At the end of the first year, you earn $50 in interest, bringing your total to $1,050. In the second year, you earn interest on the new total, not just your original $1,000.

This means you earn $52. 50, making your total $1,102. 50. Over time, this growth accelerates, demonstrating the profound impact of compound interest when left to mature.

The Time Element: Why Sooner is Better

It's worth noting that The true magic of compound interest is unveiled over time. The longer your money is invested, the greater the return will be

This simple yet powerful truth underscores the importance of starting your emergency fund early. Even modest contributions can grow substantially given enough time, thereby easing the burden of achieving your savings goals.

Consider this scenario: Imagine you start saving $1,000 a year for your emergency fund at the age of 25 with an interest rate of 5%.

By the time you reach 65, your savings will have grown to over $120,000. If you start ten years later, however, using the same rate and savings amount, the fund would only accumulate to approximately $70,000—a striking difference simply because of a decade's delay.

The Practical Approach: Finding the Right Account

To harness the power of compound interest, you need to choose the right type of account. Several accounts offer compounded interest, but they differ in terms of frequency, rates, and liquidity.

A high-yield savings account is a practical choice for most who are focusing on emergency funds due to its relatively higher interest rates compared to standard savings accounts. Look for accounts that compound interest at least monthly to optimize growth potential.

Another option is a money market account, which generally provides higher interest rates and allows some check-writing capabilities, combining the benefits of savings and checking accounts.

Some individuals might also explore certificates of deposit (CDs), which often boast higher interest rates but require funds to be locked in for designated periods.

When selecting an account, consider the interest rate, compounding frequency, any fees associated, and the level of access you might need in urgency.

Align these factors with your financial situation and risk tolerance to select the most effective option for supporting your emergency fund.

The Impact on Your Saving Strategy

Understanding and applying compound interest should be at the forefront of your saving strategy.

It's not merely about putting away what you can, but strategically placing it where it will grow the most. By prioritizing regular contributions to your emergency fund and taking advantage of higher interest accounts, you can accomplish more with less—saving smart without the need to sacrifice excessively.

Automating your savings can further enhance this strategy.

Setting up automatic transfers from your paycheck into a savings account ensures constant growth without requiring active decision-making every month. This consistency is key; with every contribution, you're amplifying your fund through compounding, gently but effectively increasing your financial cushion.

Overcoming Common Misconceptions

A common misconception is that compound interest will yield significant returns only with large sums of money.

This myth often dissuades individuals from taking advantage of this powerful tool. However, as demonstrated earlier, regular small contributions can also generate substantial returns over time, especially when invested early.

Another misconception is the lack of immediate accessibility to funds in interest-earning accounts.

While some accounts like CDs might have limitations, most high-yield savings and money market accounts provide sufficient liquidity to cover emergencies. Prioritizing accounts that allow easy access during urgent situations, while still growing your savings, unto itself harnesses the essence of a well-structured emergency fund.

Conclusion: Wrapping up Compound Interest

The power of compound interest can best be understood as a steadfast ally in your financial mobilization—a quiet yet relentless force working in your favor, amplifying the impact of your savings efforts.

The fundamental lesson here is not merely to recognize the potential of compound interest, but to act upon it, embedding it within the heart of your financial planning.

Start early, remain consistent, and choose wisely.

These key actions will allow you to capitalize on compound interest, thereby enabling you to save intelligently without undue financial strain. Remember, each dollar invested in an interest-earning account today holds the promise of a greater buffer in times of need, proving the oft-repeated maxim that it is not merely the savings that matter, but how you wield their growth potential.

It's worth noting that By mastering the principles of compound interest, you transform your emergency fund from a simple stash of cash into a robust financial shield, capable of enduring the interests of life's unpredictability.

As you move forward, let compound interest be your guide towards stability, a testament to the profound impact of informed, strategic saving.

Chapter 13: Emergency Fund vs. Investment: Knowing the Difference

Imagine standing at a crossroads, with one path leading to a secure safety net and the other promising long-term financial growth. This is often how people perceive the concepts of an emergency fund and investments.

While both elements are crucial in any personal financial strategy, understanding the distinctions between them can significantly impact how you decide to allocate your money and prepare for the future. This chapter will provide you with a practical guide to distinguishing between an emergency fund and investments, and how each can serve your financial goals without compromising the other.

The Function and Purpose

Interestingly enough, Let's start with the fundamental purposes of these financial tools. An emergency fund is akin to your financial safety net.

It is designed to cover unexpected expenses, such as medical emergencies, sudden car repairs, or even unforeseen job loss. The primary characteristic of an emergency fund is accessibility—it should be liquid, meaning you can withdraw the money quickly without incurring penalties. Typically held in high-yield savings accounts or money market accounts, an emergency fund should be easy to access yet secure from market fluctuations.

On the other hand, investments are vehicles for wealth growth. They involve committing money to assets like stocks, bonds, mutual funds, or real estate with the expectation that these assets will generate income or appreciate over time.

The key purpose of investments is to build wealth for future needs, such as retirement, education, or major life purchases. While investments have the potential to offer high returns, they also come with risks and are generally less liquid than emergency funds.

The Path to Building Each

Establishing an emergency fund is often the first step for anyone beginning to take control of their finances. Financial advisors typically recommend setting aside three to six months' worth of living expenses, held in a readily accessible account.

The emphasis is on security and preservation of capital, not on generating returns. The steps to build an emergency fund are relatively straightforward: calculate your monthly essential expenses—such as housing, utilities, groceries, and transportation—and multiply by the number of months you want to cover.

Investments, however, require a different approach. A key aspect of investing is understanding your risk tolerance and time horizon.

Depending on these factors, you can choose an appropriate asset allocation, balancing between stocks (which are riskier but offer higher potential returns) and bonds (which are generally safer but yield lower returns). With investments, you're building wealth over time, and thus, regular contributions to your investment accounts are crucial. Investing is more complex and requires ongoing education and strategy adjustments.

Liquidity and Accessibility

Let's not forget, One of the most significant differences between an emergency fund and investments is liquidity: the ability to quickly convert assets to cash without significant loss in value.

An emergency fund must be highly liquid. Since its primary role is to provide immediate financial relief, it should be stored in accounts where funds can be accessed within 24-48 hours.

Investments, however, may involve assets like equities or real estate, which are not quickly or easily liquidated without potential loss.

Selling investments can take time, and during market downturns, you might end up selling these assets at a loss. Besides, some investments have lock-in periods, where withdrawing funds early incurs penalties.

Risk and Stability

Many people don't realize this, but Risk management is where the differences between these financial tools become starkly apparent. Emergency funds are characterized by stability.

Because they are kept in insured accounts or instruments like certificates of deposit (CDs), there's virtually no risk to the principal amount. The funds retain their value and are protected against market volatility.

In contrast, investments inherently involve market risk.

Stocks can fluctuate widely based on market conditions, economic shifts, and changes within the companies themselves. While there's no denying their potential for higher returns, there's also the risk of losing your initial investment, especially if you must liquidate during a downturn.

Psychological Impact

The psychological comfort offered by having both an emergency fund and investments should not be underestimated.

Having an emergency fund provides peace of mind, knowing that unexpected financial hurdles won't throw your life— or your investments—into disarray. It's the cushion that absorbs shocks, preventing the need to disrupt your investment strategy or incur unnecessary debt.

Investments, meanwhile, offer a different kind of satisfaction: the sense of building toward a financially secure future.

Watching your investments grow can be rewarding and motivate you to continue disciplined saving and investment strategies. Balancing both aspects enables you to maintain a financial base for emergencies while also pursuing growth.

Strategic Integration

At first glance, In a balanced financial strategy, both an emergency fund and investments coexist and serve distinct, yet complementary, roles. Initially, focus on building an adequately-sized emergency fund.

Only after establishing this financial buffer should you divert excess cash toward investments. This ensures that in case of an emergency, you're not forced to dip into your investments and potentially sell them at an inopportune time.

Moreover, regularly revisit and reassess both your emergency fund and your investments.

Life circumstances change—a raise at work, a new family member, or personal financial goals—and your financial strategies should adapt in response. This reassessment might mean increasing your emergency fund, adjusting your risk tolerance, or reallocating your investment portfolio to align with new life stages or objectives.

Conclusion

To be honest, In summary, a healthy financial portfolio requires both emergency funds and investments, each serving a distinct purpose in your overall economic health.

By understanding their differences in function, structure, and strategy, you empower yourself to make informed decisions that build not just wealth, but security. Remember, the road to financial stability isn’t about choosing one path over the other; it's about paving both for a future that's fortified against the unforeseen and enriched by growth.

Chapter 14: Leveraging Technology for Smarter Savings

In today's fast-paced digital age, technology has become an integral part of our daily lives, influencing everything from how we communicate and work to how we manage our finances.

For anyone looking to build a robust emergency fund without substantial sacrifices, leveraging technology can provide effective and innovative solutions. This chapter will delve into the various technological tools and resources available to help you save smarter and more efficiently.

Understanding Financial Apps

I've seen this happen before: The advent of financial apps has revolutionized the way we save and manage money.

These apps range from budgeting tools to automated saving platforms, providing users with unprecedented control and insights into their finances.

1. Budgeting Apps:

Budgeting is the cornerstone of any savings plan. Today's budgeting apps, such as Mint, YNAB (You Need A Budget), and PocketGuard, simplify this process by linking directly to your bank accounts and credit cards.

These apps track your spending in real-time, categorize expenses, and provide you with a visual representation of your financial habits. This transparency helps identify areas where you can cut back and reallocate funds to your emergency savings. The ease of access and user-friendly interfaces of these apps make them indispensable for those committed to saving more efficiently.

2. Automated Savings Apps:

As strange as it sounds, Automated savings platforms, like Acorns, Digit, and Qapital, are designed to take the guesswork out of saving. These apps can be linked to your bank accounts and will automatically transfer small amounts of money to a savings account based on rules you set.

For example, Acorns rounds up your purchases to the nearest dollar and saves the difference. Digit analyzes your spending habits, determining when it's safe to transfer small amounts without causing you financial distress. Such automation ensures that you're consistently saving without needing to make conscious efforts each time.

Online Banking Benefits

The shift towards online banking has brought with it numerous benefits that can aid in building an emergency fund.

Let's not forget, **1. Higher Interest Rates on Online Savings Accounts:**

Many online banks offer higher interest rates on savings accounts compared to traditional brick-and-mortar banks.

Since online banks have lower overhead costs, they can pass these savings on to customers in the form of more competitive interest rates. This can significantly accelerate the growth of your emergency fund over time.

2. Sub-accounts for Different Savings Goals:

Online banking platforms often allow you to create sub-accounts, making it easier to allocate funds for multiple purposes, including an emergency fund.

Label each sub-account with specific goals and set up automatic transfers to ensure regular contributions.

3. Lower Fees:

Online banks typically have fewer fees compared to traditional banks.

By switching to or supplementing with an online bank, you can save money that would otherwise go towards maintaining accounts or paying service fees.

Advanced Budgeting with Spreadsheets

Though spreadsheets are a more traditional tool, software like Microsoft Excel or Google Sheets remains an incredibly powerful way to tailor your budgeting to personal needs. The advantage of using spreadsheets is the ability to customize everything.

You don't have to adhere to the limitations of apps. This method requires more effort initially but offers flexibility in creating formulas that can automatically update balances, track savings goals, and visualize your progress through graphs and charts.

To get started, download budget templates or use pre-built spreadsheets which often include categorized expenses, income tracking, and sections dedicated to savings.

Integrating this with your online banking data can give a real-time perspective of your financial picture. Conditional formatting, pivot tables, and complex formulas can help create a dynamic tool that caters specifically to your savings goals.

Crypto and Fintech Innovations

The rise of cryptocurrencies and financial technology (fintech) innovations has opened new avenues for saving and investment, albeit with some risks and volatility.

1. Crypto Savings Accounts:

Some platforms offer crypto savings accounts, where digital currency savings generate interest. While these can offer higher returns, they come with significant risks related to market volatility.

If you're risk-averse or unfamiliar with cryptocurrencies, it's wise to exercise caution. Ideally, use these accounts as a supplement rather than the core of your emergency fund.

2. Micro-Investing Platforms:

Micro-investing platforms provide a way to enter the investment market with very small amounts of money.

These platforms allow you to invest spare change or small sums, which can compound over time to make a significant addition to your emergency fund. By setting conservative portfolios, you can lower the risk associated with stock market investments.

Security Measures

To be honest, With increased accessibility comes the responsibility of ensuring the security of your financial data. Utilize multi-factor authentication, secure passwords, and personal banking notifications to protect your accounts.

Regularly review account statements and transactions to identify any fraudulent activity early. Familiarize yourself with the terms and conditions of the apps and services you use, and ensure they comply with financial regulations and pertinent encryption standards.

Conclusion

Leveraging technology in your savings plan is akin to having a team of expert advisors at your fingertips, ready to assist in making informed decisions and optimizing your financial health.

By thoughtfully integrating budgeting apps, online banking, spreadsheets, and fintech innovations into your financial strategy, you can build a solid emergency fund with minimal sacrifice to your lifestyle. Embrace the digital tools available, always stay informed of the latest developments, and remember the primary goal: creating a reliable financial safety net.

Chapter 15: Overcoming Common Savings Obstacles

Life is a winding path filled with unexpected detours, and while building an emergency fund is an essential financial goal, it often encounters formidable obstacles along the way.

The journey towards a robust safety net requires not only discipline but also resilience in confronting and overcoming these common savings obstacles. Let us delve into some prevalent challenges and explore practical strategies to overcome them, ensuring your emergency fund plan remains on solid ground.

1. Inconsistent Income

Many people don't realize this, but One of the most common obstacles to saving is dealing with an inconsistent income.

This issue is particularly familiar to freelancers, gig economy workers, and anyone reliant on commissions. While the unpredictability of income can make budgeting difficult, it is far from insurmountable.

Practical Tips:

- **Establish a Baseline Budget:** Determine the bare minimum monthly expenses needed to sustain your lifestyle.

This will help identify how much you absolutely need, irrespective of your fluctuating income.

It's worth noting that - **Create an Income Averaging System:** Calculate your average monthly income over six months and use this as a guide for your budget.

Set aside any surplus income during high-earning months to fill in during leaner times.

- **Emergency Fund First:** Prioritize your emergency fund as the first "bill" you pay each month, treating it with the same seriousness as rent or utilities.

2. High Living Costs

Many people don't realize this, but High living costs, especially in urban areas, can squeeze your ability to save.

However, this does not mean financial prudence is out of reach.

Practical Tips:

- **Reevaluate Housing Costs:** Consider options for reducing housing expenses, such as downsizing, house-hacking by renting out a spare room, or relocating to a more affordable neighborhood.

- **Cut Down on Utilities and Groceries:** Explore energy-saving practices to reduce utility bills, couponing, bulk buying, and meal planning to minimize grocery expenses.

- **Participate in Cost-Saving Communities:** Many online and local communities offer tips for saving money in high-cost areas.

Engaging in these can introduce you to effective savings strategies you may not have considered.

3. Lack of Financial Knowledge

It's worth noting that Embarking on a savings journey without a fundamental understanding of financial principles can be daunting.

This lack of knowledge can stall progress and create self-doubt.

Practical Tips:

- **Educate Yourself:** Start with readily available resources such as podcasts, eBooks, financial blogs, and webinars that provide actionable insights into managing money.

Interestingly enough, - **Leverage Free Courses and Workshops:** Many institutions offer free courses on personal finance, covering budgeting, saving, and investing.

- **Consult with a Financial Advisor:** If resources allow, a session with a financial advisor can offer personalized insights and set you on the right path.

4. Unexpected Expenses

As strange as it sounds, Life is riddled with surprises, and unplanned expenses can quickly deplete an emergency fund.

While it is impossible to predict every hurdle, you can cushion the blow of the unexpected.

Practical Tips:

- **Build a Buffer Fund:** In addition to your main emergency fund, maintain a smaller buffer fund for minor unexpected expenses.

This reduces the frequency of dipping into the main fund.

At first glance, - **Regular Maintenance Purchases:** Regularly service your car, home appliances, and devices to prevent larger, more expensive breakdowns.

- **Insurance Policies:** Evaluate your insurance policies to ensure they cover essential aspects of your life, providing a safety net for major unexpected events.

5. Behavioral Barriers

Believe it or not, Sometimes, our own behaviors, such as impulsive spending or procrastination, can be the biggest obstacles to saving.

Practical Tips:

- **Set S.M.A.R.T Goals:** Specific, Measurable, Achievable, Relevant, and Time-bound goals provide a clear vision and impactful motivation, minimizing impulsive tendencies.

Believe it or not, - **Automate Savings:** Set up automatic transfers from your checking account to your savings account.

This diminishes the temptation to spend money that should be saved.

- **Mindful Spending:** Before making a purchase, impose a waiting period. This breaks the cycle of impulsivity and fosters more intentional spending habits.

6. Social Pressures

I've seen this happen before: The pressure to keep up with peers can lead to overspending, detracting from your savings goals.

However, maintaining focus on your financial well-being is paramount.

Practical Tips:

- **Set Personal Priorities:** Reflect on your values and prioritize financial security over fleeting societal validation.

In real life, - **Communicate with Peers:** Open conversations about budgetary limits can foster an understanding among friends and family.

- **Suggest Affordable Alternatives:** Propose budget-friendly social activities that allow you to maintain relationships without financial strain.

7. Low Income

It's worth noting that Feeling restricted by a low income can be disheartening, but it need not be an impassable barrier.

Practical Tips:

- **Supplement Your Income:** Consider side gigs or freelance work that fits your skill set and schedule.

In real life, - **Utilize Government Assistance Programs:** Explore available programs designed to support those with low incomes in achieving financial stability.

- **Enhance Skills:** Invest time in gaining new skills that could increase your earning potential through raises, promotions, or new job opportunities.

In conclusion, while saving for an emergency fund has its challenges, a robust strategy can address and overcome these obstacles. Remember, the key is persistence and adaptability.

By anticipating roadblocks and equipping yourself with practical solutions, your journey to a secure financial future will be successful and rewarding. The path to financial resilience is not about avoidance—it's about overcoming and adapting, securing peace of mind, and creating a buffer against the uncertainties of life.

Chapter 16: Staying Motivated on Your Savings Journey

Embarking on the journey to build an emergency fund is a commendable step towards financial security. However, staying motivated to consistently save money is often easier said than done.

Life throws curveballs, and unexpected expenses can sap your momentum and determination. Yet, keeping motivation high is crucial to building a robust financial safety net. This chapter is your guide to nurturing the persistence and resilience needed to achieve your savings goals.

Understand Your "Why"

As strange as it sounds, To maintain motivation, it's important to have a clear understanding of why you're saving. Your "why" serves as the guiding star that directs your efforts when the journey gets tough.

Is it to avoid debt during unplanned emergencies? Or perhaps to create peace of mind knowing that you have a financial cushion? Write down your reasons and keep them visible—on a sticky note at your workstation, on your fridge, or as a reminder on your phone. Revisiting your "why" regularly can keep you anchored and committed to your goal.

Set Achievable Milestones

Long-term goals can seem daunting, which is why it's beneficial to break them down into smaller, more manageable objectives. For instance, instead of fixating on a goal of saving $10,000 over a few years, set interim targets such as saving the first $1,000 in three months.

Celebrate each milestone as you reach it. Acknowledging small victories can boost your morale and propel you forward.

Make Savings Automatic

One of the most effective ways to stay on track is to make saving money an automatic process. Set up a system where a portion of your income is transferred directly to your savings account as soon as you receive your paycheck.

This way, savings become a non-negotiable part of your budget, reducing the temptation to spend it elsewhere. Automatic savings diminish the mental burden and decision fatigue, allowing you to stay motivated with minimal daily effort.

Engage With Your Support Network

Sharing your goals with trusted friends or family can provide the accountability that fuels motivation.

Discussing your progress, challenges, and plans not only strengthens your commitment but also opens avenues for encouragement and advice. More so, consider joining financial forums or local support groups where you can share experiences, learn new strategies, and celebrate successes together.

Visualize Your Progress

Humans are inherently visual creatures, and seeing tangible proof of progress can be incredibly motivating. Consider using a visual tracker, like a graph or a chart, where you can record your savings growth over time.

Some utilize jars with color-coded beads or digital apps with graphical displays. Watching your efforts materialize can give a substantial boost to your motivation, turning abstract numbers into something you see evolving.

Create a Rewards System

Yes, saving is rewarding in itself, but introducing a system where you reward yourself after reaching certain targets can add an extra layer of motivation.

These rewards don't have to be extravagant; they can be as simple as a movie night, a book purchase, or a small outing with friends. Associating rewards with your savings goals creates positive reinforcement, making the journey more enjoyable and less of a chore.

Focus on Financial Education

Let's not forget, Continuing to educate yourself about personal finance can also keep your motivation levels high.

Books, podcasts, seminars, and webinars about money management can offer fresh perspectives, introduce you to new tactics, and help you stay enthusiastic about achieving your financial goals. Knowledge is empowering and serves as a constant reminder of why your efforts will pay off in the long run.

Embrace Flexibility

Life is unpredictable, and setting rigid plans can sometimes backfire, causing frustration when things don't go as expected. Allow room for flexibility in your savings plan

If an unavoidable expense arises, adjust your strategy temporarily without guilt. Being adaptable will prevent you from feeling disheartened, helping you to return to your savings track with renewed vigor when circumstances stabilize.

Reflect and Reassess Regularly

Make it a habit to review your financial strategy at regular intervals. Evaluate what's working well and what might need tweaking.

Reflecting on your progress—noting how each deposit no matter how small, brings you one step closer to your goal—can fortify your resolve. Reassessing and adjusting as necessary keeps your plan aligned with your evolving financial situation and personal priorities.

Cultivate a Positive Mindset

Many people don't realize this, but Finally, embracing a positive mindset is key to sustaining motivation. Instead of focusing on sacrifices or what you might be missing out on, concentrate on the gains you're achieving—and the security and opportunities that will emerge from having a solid financial foundation.

Celebrate effort, not perfection. Remember, building an emergency fund is not just about accumulating money; it's about cultivating stability and resilience in your life.

Saving for an emergency fund is a marathon, not a sprint.

Staying motivated is about maintaining a steady pace, adapting to the turns along the way, and keeping an eye on the finish line. By understanding the value of persistence, leveraging strategic planning, and celebrating each step forward, you'll not only reach your savings goals but build a foundation of confidence and control over your financial future.

Chapter 17: Adjusting Your Plan for Life Changes

Life is an unpredictable journey, filled with twists and turns that can challenge even the most meticulously crafted financial plans. Despite our best efforts to forecast and prepare, changes in our life circumstances can demand an adjustment to our financial strategies.

Whether it's a career shift, expanding your family, or moving to a new city, these changes can significantly impact your financial landscape. Therefore, it's crucial to remain adaptable and revisit your emergency fund plan to ensure it continues to serve your needs effectively.

Recognizing the Need for Change

Let's not forget, Acknowledging that your emergency fund plan requires evaluation is the first and most crucial step. Major life events such as marriage, the birth of a child, divorce, or even the bittersweet reality of retirement, come with financial implications that might necessitate a reassessment of your savings strategy.

For instance, welcoming a new baby into the family brings joy but also new expenses, from healthcare to education savings. Similarly, if you find yourself transitioning into a different career, your income stability may be temporarily affected, requiring adjustments to your current financial safety net.

Likewise, inflation, changing economic conditions, or an unforeseen medical crisis can demand a shift in how much you save.

Periodically reviewing your plan ensures you're not caught off guard. It's beneficial to schedule a yearly financial review, much like an annual health check-up, to examine whether your fund still aligns with your goals and lifestyle.

Assessing Your Current Situation

Once you've identified the need for a change, take stock of your current financial situation. This involves a thorough review of income, expenses, debts, and existing savings.

Begin by examining your budget to address shifting priorities. If your income has changed, whether increased or decreased, reflect that in your length and amount of emergency fund coverage. A common recommendation is to have three to six months' worth of expenses saved, but life changes might require you to revise this benchmark.

For example, if you're moving to a city with a higher cost of living, it's prudent to adjust your emergency fund goal upward. On the other hand, finding a more stable or lucrative position than before might allow you to build your fund at a faster rate.

Use this opportunity to scrutinize fixed and variable expenses to determine new financial obligations. Ensure to account for any additional insurance coverage, healthcare expenses, or school tuition if your circumstances warrant this.

Resetting Your Emergency Fund Goals

With a clear picture of your current situation in hand, redefine your emergency fund goals. Begin by recalculating your essential monthly expenses and identify a new target amount.

This figure should accommodate both your existing and anticipated living costs. Consider practical adjustments, for instance, if you have a growing family or an aging parent to care for, you might want to set aside more than six months of expenses.

In determining your monthly savings goal to reach this target, be realistic about what you can consistently contribute without compromising your current lifestyle.

Automate your savings to help maintain discipline and ensure that the new goal becomes part of your routine.

Balancing Risk with Prudence

As you modify your plan, it's imperative to balance risk against available resources prudently.

If you've recently taken on additional financial burdens, such as a home mortgage, it's essential to assess how this impacts your cash flow and risk tolerance. Review any investments or liabilities you have, as increased risk may require a larger cushion to protect against downturns.

Furthermore, consider any insurance policies that might offset potential emergencies, such as health, disability, or life insurance.

The coverage from these policies could reduce the size of the emergency fund you need to account for specific scenarios, allowing you more freedom to adjust how much you set aside.

Making the Adjustments Practical

It's worth noting that Once your new plan is in place, integrate it seamlessly into your everyday life. This involves not only adhering to new savings commitments but also addressing any habits that could impede progress.

Minimize unnecessary or impulsive spending and redirect discretionary funds into your emergency savings account. It might also be an ideal time to explore additional income avenues, such as freelance work or part-time opportunities, to boost savings.

Moreover, keep channels for emergency fund contributions flexible and adaptive to change.

Life is fluid, and your financial plan should be too. If strain from your current savings plan becomes apparent, do not hesitate to slightly lower contributions momentarily but ensure it remains a short-term solution rather than a new norm.

Maintaining Accountability

It's worth noting that Consistent monitoring is essential to ensure that your revised emergency fund plan remains effective.

Establish benchmarks and track your progress over time, making adjustments as necessary. This could involve using financial apps that help manage your budget, reminding you of savings milestones, or even consulting a financial advisor for professional guidance.

Also, engage your family or any financial partner in the process.

Sharing your goals and challenges provides added support and accountability, reinforcing the commitment to maintaining a healthy financial safety net.

Preparing for Future Changes

In real life, Lastly, while you've adjusted for the current life changes, keep the mindset that future adjustments might be necessary.

Building flexibility into your emergency fund plan prepares you for life's unpredictability. Always saving a little beyond your target can create an additional buffer for the uncertain events ahead.

By learning to adapt your emergency fund plan with life's evolving circumstances, you not only safeguard your financial future but also cultivate resilience against the unexpected.

This proactive approach ensures that your financial health is robust enough to support your needs, no matter what life throws your way.

Chapter 18: Maintaining Your Emergency Fund: Best Practices

As you stand on the precipice of genuine financial security, the importance of maintaining your emergency fund cannot be overstated. You've put in the hard work, made sacrifices, and now possess a fund that can shield you against life's unpredictable curveballs.

However, like any other aspect of financial management, your emergency fund requires ongoing attention and care to ensure it remains robust and effective. In this chapter, we'll explore the best practices for maintaining your emergency fund, ensuring it serves its purpose without compromise.

Regular Monitoring: Keep the Pulse

As strange as it sounds, Just as you routinely check your bank account balance or investment portfolio, monitoring your emergency fund should become a habit.

Regular reviews of your fund serve multiple purposes: they allow you to track progress, ensure alignment with your goals, and provide early warning for any potential issues.

Set a monthly or quarterly schedule to review your fund. During this check-in, ask yourself:

As strange as it sounds, - Is the fund's balance reflecting lower than expected due to unforeseen expenses?

- Have there been any changes in your financial situation, such as increased monthly expenses, that might necessitate adjusting the size of the fund?

- Are there any upcoming life changes, like a new job or a family addition, that require recalibrating your fund?

The key is to keep your fund dynamic, reacting not only to emergencies but also to shifts in your life circumstances.

Automated Savings: Keep the Flow Consistent

Automating contributions to your emergency fund can be one of the most effective ways to maintain and grow it with minimal effort.

Set up an automatic transfer from your primary account to your emergency fund account every time you receive a paycheck. This ensures that saving becomes a consistent practice, helping you maintain your fund without having to rely on willpower alone.

Consider using round-up savings apps that automatically save the difference every time you make a purchase.

These small, incremental savings can accumulate over time, contributing to your emergency fund with ease.

Periodic Fund Replenishment: Stay Prepared

Even with a well-maintained fund, life will inevitably throw a curveball resulting in you dipping into your emergency reserves. What's crucial is how you respond after utilizing these funds.

Replenishment should be immediate and prioritized. Once the emergency has passed, create a plan to restore your fund to its pre-emergency state. Treat this task with urgency, ensuring that your safety net is fully operational for the next unexpected event.

Income Boosting: Enhance Your Reserves

It's worth noting that Augment your emergency fund with extra income beyond your regular job.

Whether it's freelance work, a side hustle, or selling items you no longer need, funnel these extra funds directly into your emergency savings. This practice not only speeds up the replenishment process after an emergency but also strengthens your financial buffer more rapidly in ordinary times.

Avoid Temptation: Keep the Fund Exclusive

Your emergency fund's purpose is singular: to shield you from unforeseen financial shocks. Hence, it is vital to resist the temptation to dip into this fund for non-emergencies.

Vacations, new gadgets, or luxury expenditures should not rely on your emergency resources. To help maintain this boundary, keep your emergency fund in a separate account, preferably one that's not easily accessible with your standard debit card. This separation can instill a mental barrier and deter impulsive spending.

To be honest, #### Inflation Adjustments: Preserve Purchasing Power

An often-overlooked aspect of maintaining an emergency fund is adjusting for inflation. Over time, inflation can erode the purchasing power of your savings, meaning that a fund adequate today might not be sufficient in the years to come.

Periodically assess your fund in the context of inflation rates and increase your savings accordingly. Staying proactive with these adjustments ensures that when you face an emergency, the funds are enough to handle what they were initially intended for.

Account Selection: Optimize Your Savings

As strange as it sounds, Where you store your emergency fund matters. Choose a savings account that offers high interest yet easy access in times of need.

Online banks frequently provide more competitive interest rates than traditional brick-and-mortar institutions. However, avoid tying your emergency fund into accounts where withdrawals are limited or penalized, such as CDs or certain investment accounts, as emergencies often demand immediate access to cash.

Mindful Budgeting: Align Expenses with Goals

Continuous budgeting ensures that your expenditure behaviors align with the goal of maintaining and growing your emergency fund.

Regularly review your budget to find areas where you can cut costs without compromising your lifestyle. It's these incremental adjustments in your spending that can foster the growth of your emergency fund without feeling like a financial sacrifice.

Professional Advice: Seek Guidance

Consider periodically consulting with a financial advisor to ensure your emergency fund strategy remains sound.

A professional can provide insights tailored to your specific financial situation and help strategize ways to both protect and enhance your fund in line with your long-term financial plans.

By incorporating these best practices into your financial routine, you safeguard your emergency fund against negligence and shortsightedness.

It will remain a steadfast guardian against the uncertainties of life, allowing peace of mind and financial stability as you navigate your journey. Your dedication today in maintaining this fund ensures you're well-equipped for whatever tomorrow may bring.

Chapter 19: When and How to Use Your Emergency Fund

Building an emergency fund is a crucial step towards financial security, but understanding when and how to appropriately use this fund is equally important.

An emergency fund is not a routine bank account; it is a financial safety net designed to protect you from life's unexpected financial surprises. In this chapter, we will explore the appropriate circumstances under which to use your emergency fund and provide practical guidance on how to access these savings without jeopardizing your financial future.

Identifying a True Emergency

As strange as it sounds, First, let's define what qualifies as a true emergency.

A financial emergency is typically unexpected, necessary, and urgent. These criteria help differentiate genuine emergencies from regular expenses or foreseen financial obligations.

1. **Unexpected**: Emergencies are unplanned events.

If you can anticipate an expense, it is not a candidate for your emergency fund. For instance, car maintenance should be budgeted as a regular expense, but sudden car repairs due to an accident qualify as unexpected.

2. **Necessary**: The expense must be essential to your life or well-being.

Medical emergencies, for instance, are necessary, but a sale on a luxury item is not. Consider whether the situation significantly impacts your health, livelihood, or safety.

It's worth noting that 3.

Urgent: An emergency requires immediate attention. Delaying the payment could result in severe consequences, such as losing your home or worsening a health condition.

Common Scenarios for Using Your Emergency Fund

Now that we've established what constitutes an emergency, let's look at some common scenarios where tapping into your emergency fund is justified:

Let's not forget, - **Job Loss**: Losing your primary source of income is a significant financial shock.

Your emergency fund can cover living expenses while you search for a new job. It's crucial, however, to prioritize essentials like rent, utilities, and groceries to preserve your fund until your financial situation stabilizes.

- **Major Health Expenses**: Despite having health insurance, unexpected medical bills can be substantial.

Your emergency fund can help you manage large out-of-pocket expenses, ensuring you receive necessary care without sinking into debt.

- **Urgent Home Repairs**: A burst pipe or a failing roof can cause substantial damage if not addressed promptly.

Emergency funds should cover the immediate, essential repairs that prevent further damage and safeguard your living situation.

Believe it or not, - **Car Repairs**: If your car is your primary means of transportation and essential for work or other responsibilities, emergency funds might be needed for major unplanned repairs.

- **Family Emergencies**: Situations like funerals, or the sudden need to travel to care for a family member, can be financially burdensome.

Your emergency fund is there to alleviate these unexpected costs.

How to Access Your Emergency Fund

Interestingly enough, Accessing your emergency fund should be straightforward but not too easy, to prevent impulsive decisions.

Here are practical steps for how to use your fund wisely:.

1.

Evaluate the Situation: Before withdrawing money, assess the situation against the criteria of unexpected, necessary, and urgent. Consider alternative solutions, such as negotiating payment plans, to see if the full amount from your fund is truly needed.

2.

Determine the Required Amount: Once you've confirmed the situation is an emergency, calculate the minimum amount required to cover the expense. Avoid withdrawing more than necessary to keep the remainder of your fund intact.

It's worth noting that 3. **Document the Withdrawal**: Keep thorough records of any withdrawals.

This creates accountability and helps you track and understand where your emergency funds are being used. It also aids in refocusing your efforts to replenish the fund.

4.

Prioritize Repayment: After resolving the emergency, create a plan to replenish your fund as quickly as possible. Consider increasing temporary savings or cutting non-essential expenses until the fund is restored.

5.

Reflect and Adjust: Post-emergency, evaluate whether your fund is still adequate. If you find that an unexpected expense depleted your savings more than anticipated, consider increasing the fund target for future security.

Tips to Prevent Unnecessary Withdrawals

Maintaining the integrity of your emergency fund is vital to your long-term financial health. Here are some tips to avoid misuse:

- **Create a Specific Emergency Fund Account**: Keep your emergency savings in a dedicated account separate from your regular checking or savings accounts.

Consider using a high-yield savings account to earn interest while keeping the funds accessible.

- **Avoid Debit Cards Linked to the Account**: To minimize the temptation of instant spending, do not link a debit card to your emergency fund.

Ensure accessing the funds requires deliberate effort, such as transferring to a main account or visiting a bank.

- **Budget for Non-Emergencies**: Anticipate irregular expenses like home maintenance and gifts by building them into your monthly budget.

This separates day-to-day finances from emergencies and reduces the temptation to misuse the fund.

- **Communicate Financial Boundaries**: If you share finances with family or a partner, establish clear guidelines about what constitutes an emergency to ensure consistent and disciplined use of the fund.

Conclusion

Using your emergency fund wisely is an exercise in discipline, prioritization, and strategic decision-making.

Knowing when and how to use this financial safety net is as crucial as building it, helping sustain your financial health across unforeseen setbacks. By adhering to the principles and practices outlined in this chapter, you equip yourself with the knowledge to handle financial emergencies confidently, ensuring your fund serves its intended purpose without compromising your future stability.

Chapter 20: Conclusion: Achieving Financial Resilience

As we reach the culmination of our journey towards creating a robust emergency fund, it is essential to reflect on the key components of financial resilience.

Building financial security through an emergency fund is not merely about setting aside a portion of your income. It is a deliberate strategy to safeguard your financial well-being and ensure stability in the face of unforeseen circumstances.

Financial resilience starts with a shift in mindset. It requires adopting a proactive attitude towards money management, where planning and preparedness become foundational aspects of your daily life.

It's about expecting the unexpected and equipping yourself to handle life's curveballs without derailing your financial stability. The process of building an emergency fund is an exercise in discipline, commitment, and continuous awareness of one's financial goals and priorities.

One crucial element of financial resilience is understanding the role of an emergency fund. Instead of viewing it as an onerous obligation or a safety net for worst-case scenarios, consider it a financial lifeline.

An emergency fund is not simply a tool; it is a buffer that provides peace of mind, allowing you to address emergencies with confidence. When you have a fund in place, you are empowered to make decisions that best suit your situation without the added burden of financial stress.

In this journey, striking a balance has been central. You have learned that saving smartly does not mean sacrificing your current lifestyle drastically.

Instead, it involves a series of informed, calculated adjustments that enable you to consistently contribute to your fund while continuing to meet your day-to-day needs. Financial resilience does not require giving up your daily coffee or denying yourself small pleasures. It is built through thoughtful budgeting, prioritization, and the careful allocation of resources.

Regularly revisiting and adjusting your budget is essential for maintaining financial resilience. Budgeting is not a one-time activity but a dynamic process that reflects your changing circumstances and financial goals.

As you grow in your career, experience changes in lifestyle, or face new challenges, your ability to adapt your budget will ensure that your emergency fund remains a priority. Embrace the habit of reviewing your financial situation regularly, and be flexible in making necessary changes to stay on track.

Moreover, diversifying your savings and exploring multiple income streams can further enhance your financial resilience.

Relying solely on a single source of income can be precarious, placing you at greater risk in the event of job loss or economic downturns. By seeking alternative income streams, such as freelance work, investments, or passive income opportunities, you can strengthen your financial foundation and expedite the growth of your emergency fund.

Another vital aspect of financial resilience is the cultivation of a healthy relationship with money. This involves recognizing and addressing emotional spending habits that may undermine your saving efforts.

Mindful spending, where purchases are made consciously and with purpose, ensures that your financial resources are directed towards building long-term security rather than transient satisfactions. Developing financial literacy and seeking knowledge continuously will bolster your decision-making and empower you to make wise financial choices.

Financial resilience is also about leveraging the available resources to maximize your efficiency in building an emergency fund. We explored various tools and techniques throughout this book, including automated savings, high-yield savings accounts, and budgeting apps.

Each tool provides a distinct advantage, and utilizing them in combination can streamline your saving efforts and amplify your results. By integrating technology and financial tools into your strategy, you create a seamless path toward achieving your emergency fund goals.

Even as you grow your fund, remain vigilant about protecting it. Circumstances can tempt you to dip into your emergency fund for non-emergency expenses.

Remember, financial resilience requires discipline and an unwavering commitment to the fund's purpose. Establish boundaries to safeguard your fund and foster accountability to ensure its availability when you genuinely need it.

Building strong financial resilience also means anticipating potential financial risks. Consider potential scenarios such as healthcare emergencies, unexpected repairs, or unplanned family issues.

By identifying these risks and planning for them, you can avoid being caught off-guard and proactively protect your financial position. Increasing your financial literacy—whether through reading, courses, or workshops—will help you recognize risks and create a proactive plan.

Lastly, financial resilience is an ongoing journey, not a destination. It requires constant vigilance, adaptability, and learning.

Be patient with yourself, celebrate milestones along the way, and remain focused on the bigger picture. Your emergency fund is essential, but it is one of many tools that contributes to a comprehensive financial strategy. Keep honing your skills, remain open to change, and continuously evaluate and recalibrate your financial plans to fit your evolving needs.

As you conclude this book, empower yourself with the knowledge, tools, and mindset necessary to achieve financial resilience. May the principles outlined herein guide you toward a secure and resilient financial future.

The path to financial resilience is often challenging, but it is undoubtedly rewarding. With a well-structured emergency fund and a resilient financial strategy, you are well on your way to a life of stability, security, and peace of mind. Let this be your launchpad to financial empowerment, and embrace the freedom that comes with being financially prepared for whatever life throws your way.

About the Author

T. S. AVINI is a writer who believes in the power of sharing life's lessons. Having faced hardship and pain, he turned to writing as a form of self-expression and healing. Today, he pours his heart into every book, aiming to help others navigate their own struggles and find strength in vulnerability.